CELTIC WALES

T he Celts were a fair-haired Aryan race who came out of the east, probably from the Danube basin, around 1,000 years before the birth of Christ. They are first mentioned in Greek writings of 500 BC, being described as a group of tribes with a common culture. By 300 BC they were the dominant race of the western world, having imposed their Iron Age culture from the Bosphorus to the Atlantic, from the Baltic to the Mediterranean. However, they never established an empire but remained a grouping of warlike tribes, connected by a family of languages and a polytheist religion with its druidical priesthood.

The first traces of the Celts in Britain date back to 300 BC, but they had certainly started colonizing these islands before then. Their domination of Europe ended with Caesar's Gallic wars, and in Britain, following the Roman conquest of 43–85 AD, the Celtic nobility became Romanized and in places retained some local administration on behalf of the occupying power. They regained control of Britain briefly when the Romans left over 300 years later, and established the early Celtic Christian church. But they were then displaced by the pagan Anglo-Saxons. In the hills and valleys of what is now Wales, something of their culture and language – which developed into Welsh – still survives.

THE CELTS ARRIVE IN WALES

Beside the road over the hills between Tonypandy and Hirwaen in south Wales lies Llyn Fawr, an insignificant little lake but of paramount importance in the chronology of Celtic Wales. It was in the depths of this lake that an iron sword and a sickle were found in 1908. A modest find indeed, but the sword was identified as belonging to the Celtic Hallstatt culture and dated c.600 BC. Hallstatt, near Salzburg in Austria, is where a number of funerary objects, particularly chariots and harness, were discovered, and from them the name Hallstatt has been given to the advanced Iron Age culture of Celtic tribes with superior weapons who had migrated south and west from eastern Europe.

The Llyn Fawr find raises the curtain on the Celtic Iron Age in the west of Britain, Wales having no separate identity at that time. Most of the country was still in the Bronze Age, although Celts from Europe with their iron skills were beginning to settle in south-east England. It is most likely that the Iron Age technology of the Hallstatt period came to Wales via the Atlantic coastal route from France or Spain. In those days it was easier to travel by sea than through the almost impenetrable forests that covered most of Europe and Britain. Tribes living on the coast of the west country and Wales would be familiar with the cultures of mainland Europe through traders and immigrants from what is now Brittany, whereas those living well inland would have little if any knowledge of the world beyond their own territory. It would be at least three centuries before iron was in common use throughout Britain, by which time a more advanced culture was arriving from the European mainland, that of the La Tène Celts, named after a small village beside Lake Neuchâtel in Switzerland from which a rich hoard of votive offerings was recovered. The La Tène tribal chiefs were warlike and bent on expansion, but they supported the craftsmen who produced exquisitely wrought weapons, chariot decorations, harness, domestic utensils and what today would be called expensive costume jewellery. It was the culture that produced the elaborate gold torques or neck ornaments which denoted rank and social status and were later adopted by the Romans as a form of military decoration. La Tène art was embraced by a growing Celtic aristocracy, and before long local schools of metalworkers were producing some of the finest work of the period. In fact this art form with its now familiar geometric forms and stylized symbols continued to flourish in Britain after it had declined in Europe and a large number of beautiful examples have been found throughout Wales.

Right
The remains of Cytiau'r Gwyddelod Iron Age hut circle on the side of Holyhead Mountain, Anglesey.

Above
Detail of a Celtic wrought-iron firedog dating from the 1st century BC.

Below
Llyn Mymbyr with Snowdon in the background. Lakes were sacred to the Celts and many objects have been found in old lake beds.

CELTIC LIFE

Right

The enamelled bronze cat's head handle of the Gwynedd Bowl in the National Museum of Wales dates from the 1st century AD.

Below

Reconstructed Celtic huts and (inset) a raised granary, Castell Henllys, Nevern. Pigs, cattle, sheep, ducks, geese and chickens were kept and farming was efficient enough for the Roman army to have no problems with food supply when it arrived in Britain.

For a picture of what the ancient Celts looked like we must take the word of the classical writers who describe them as being tall, blond and muscular with elaborate hairstyles and, among the warrior class, big walrus moustaches. Flattering and perhaps accurate of the chiefs and noblemen, about whom the writers might have had first-hand knowledge, but archaeological finds point to anatomies more in keeping with the mixed racial characteristics to be expected following several hundred years of trans-European wanderings. The average lifespan for men was 30 years and 20 years for women. Having married at around 14 years of age, women often died in childbirth, and 50 per cent of children died before they reached 12 years old. Skeletons show that most men had suffered wounds and were prone to arthritis.

The Iron Age Celts in Wales built themselves round, thatched houses whose walls would be wattle and daub in the lowlands and drystone in highland areas. The houses were grouped together within a circular rampart topped by a pallisade or by a substantial stone wall, and always had an outer ditch – more to deter wild animals and thieves than for military defence. Hay was stacked on wooden platforms with a single pole core, and grain stored in wickerwork granaries on stilts or in pits. Outside the settlement animals grazed in fields protected by wattle fencing or deep ditches. There

would have been clamps for firing pottery and for charcoal; charcoal was used for smelting copper with tin or lead to make bronze. The metalworker was a highly respected member of the community, ranking with warriors who depended on him for their weapons, and the law stipulated that he be given the first drink at feasts.

After the 5th century BC the Celts had iron-shod ploughs capable of tackling heavy soil, and they worked their fields to get high yields. As well as wheat and rye, they grew barley for brewing beer, which was an everyday drink, although a lot of imported wine was drunk by the nobility and the wealthy. They also cultivated rape for its oil, hemp, flax and a variety of vegetables. Meat and a form of porridge would have been a staple part of their diet. They heated brine to produce blocks of salt to preserve their food. Excavations of rubbish pits have revealed that hunted animals accounted for only one to two per cent of bones, which would suggest that stock breeding was well advanced.

Tribal chiefs were elected from among the noble families, and land belonged to the tribe although it could be leased out. Only freemen had the protection of the law and were permitted to take part in tribal assemblies. Under them were the unfree who worked as bondsmen and were not permitted to own animals or property; they were actually little better than slaves who were a major factor in the Celtic economy. Although it was a patrilinear society, women had virtual equal rights; they could inherit and they could and did rule, as did Boudicca (Boadicea) for example. The nobility often had concubines, and children were routinely fostered out with families of a higher social standing to be educated and then returned to their families – a practice that created close family alliances. Prestige and rank were equated with the acquisition of property – a very good incentive for plunder!

Above
The hearth in a reconstructed hut at Castell Henllys, Nevern, Pembrokeshire. A clay oven would stand beside the open fire, its smoke percolating through the thatch.

Below
The Cytiau'r Gwyddelod Iron Age hut circle on Anglesey was occupied from the 2nd–4th century AD. About 24 huts survive from a much larger settlement.

THE DRUIDS

Below
Cefn Coch, a Bronze Age stone circle at the top of Penmaenmawr Mountain, Conwy, commonly known as the Druids' Circle. Although built long before the time of the Druids, they may have adopted it for their religious ceremonies. The Druids were also astronomers and they calculated the calendars that ordered the religious and agricultural cycles.

The Celts are said to have had 4,000 gods and goddesses, although many would be the same deities with different local names. They were the spirits of the natural world – the sky, stars, sea, rivers, lakes, springs and wells, mountains, forests and even individual trees – and they lived in those places, not in some remote heaven, so everything surrounding the Celts was sacred. Their gods talked to the Druids, the priestly caste, to whom they made known their voracious appetite for sacrifices of animals, precious objects and humans. Without sacrifices nothing could be achieved – neither health, wealth nor happiness, not fertility of man or harvest, and certainly not victory in battle. And therein lay the power of the Druids for they, and only

they, could speak with the gods and knew the secrets of the sacred rituals.

Recruited almost exclusively from among the nobility, they were the fount of all contemporary knowledge and, to protect their power, they forbade any written language. As all knowledge was committed to memory, it took 20 years of learning to become a Druid. To enable such prodigious feats of memory, everything was codified in verse, so all Druids were bards. Not all bards became Druids however, although they were part of the same privileged circle of poets, storytellers and musicians who delivered the orations, sang the praises of chiefs and warriors, and the lamentations over battles lost and the deaths of chiefs. The Druids' sanctuaries were in natural settings such as caves and forest groves

A solid gold Celtic torque found in Ireland. The gold trade was probably organized from Wales by the Druids.

well off the beaten track where they could perform their rituals unobserved. They also built temples for public worship, but almost nothing of them has been found.

It is now believed that the Druids controlled the trade in gold which passed through Wales on its way from the Wicklow Hills on the Holy Island (Ireland) to the east coast and thence over the North Sea to Europe. The famous Lindow Man, whose head and torso were found in the peat of Lindow Moss in 1984, is believed to have been a Celtic prince from Ireland who crossed the sea to offer himself as a sacrifice when the Romans were threatening Anglesey. He arrived too late, but was smuggled to Lindow, an important point on the gold route also under threat from the Romans, where he was sacrificed to protect the Druids' interests. Unusually, he was buried without his sword or other possessions and the theory is that he had deposited them as a votive offering in Llyn Cerrig Bach, a holy lake now under the runway at RAF Valley. When the airfield was under construction in 1943 more than 100 artefacts were recovered from the lake, among them chariot parts, slave chains, weapons, tools, cauldrons and trumpets along with bones of domestic animals. These finds support the belief that Anglesey was the centre of the druidic religion in Britain. By preaching the transmigration of souls, the Druids instilled into every warrior the belief that when he died he would be born again in another body, so in battle they had no fear of death – which made them recklessly brave. For this reason the Romans, normally sympathetic to tribal religions, went out of their way to destroy the Druids, and finally did so when they invaded Anglesey in 61 AD and razed their sacred groves.

Right
The peat-preserved head and torso of Lindow Man found in Cheshire.

Left
Hendy Head, a limestone head of an Iron Age Celtic god found on Anglesey.

Below
Puffin Island off Anglesey. Anglesey was the centre of the Druidic religion.

EARLY CELTIC ART

Right

A bronze bull's head ornament. The gold-smiths and enamellers, who made jewellery and who embellished scab-bards, shields, sword hilts and helmets, were highly regarded in Celtic society.

Below

Detail of a bronze shield mount, part of a hoard found at Tal-y-Llyn, Gwynedd, dating from the 1st century AD.

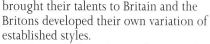

he Celts had no written language so they can speak to us today only through the work of their artists and craftsmen. Fortunately, despite being of a lively, aggressive, even bibulous disposition, they had a fine appreciation of beautiful things and their creative skills were far above those of the indigenous peoples they colonized. The exciting art styles with which weapons, luxury goods and even domestic utensils were embellished wherever the Celtic influence took hold reached Britain about the 4th century BC when the local chiefs became wealthy enough to adopt the lifestyle of their continental cousins. It was a time of great mobility, not least because of the expansion of the Roman empire, which was pressing on the Celtic tribes of Europe. Successive waves of immigrants

brought their talents to Britain and the Britons developed their own variation of established styles.

Celtic art – from the La Tène period through to the Roman occupation of Britain and, to some extent, into the early Christian era – was largely abstract in form but depicted nature: plants, animals, birds, the elements and life forces. The swirling and interwoven lines of their decorative motifs, much of them requiring skill with the compass, often had a magical or spiritual meaning which is hard for the uninitiated to comprehend. But it certainly gave a dynamic force to their art, not unlike their poetry which the Greek Diodorus described as 'brief, enigmatic, with frequent recourse to implied meaning'.

With no literature of their own, poetry was an essential art form by which their history, laws and the culture were passed down from one generation to another, their leaders and heroes praised and the people inspired. The complex and changing patterns of rhythm and alliteration in Celtic poetry add to the beauty and mystery of the words, making it most appealing to the ear. It is a poetic form which has survived with little change and can still be heard in Wales today at festivals known as eisteddfodau.

Art was part of their everyday life and was applied to everything – pottery, household utensils, jewellery and especially to harness, chariots, armour and weapons. The blacksmith, as artist in metal, was held in the highest regard and even had his own god, Gafannon. Goldsmiths and enamel workers, who embellished scabbards, shields, sword hilts and helmets, were also granted high status and ranked with poets, story-tellers and musicians. Both men and women were fond of jewellery, and wore ornamental belts and brooches. Nobles wore amber and glass beads and bracelets, and beautifully chased torques of bronze, silver or gold with sculpted terminals. The amber came from Poland and Jutland; jet, which was also worn, came from Northumbria.

Little is known of the Celts' music; it was medieval times before it was written down, but from archaeological remains we know that the lyre and some forms of wind instrument – possible ancestors of the hornpipe – were played as well as the great horns sounded in battle. The lyre would normally accompany the recitation of poetry.

The invention of the pottery wheel and their love of wine were together responsible for some very fine ceramic ware. Fierce the Celtic chief and his warriors may have looked, but they were not without artistic taste. Even the complex geometric patterns with which they painted their bodies before going into battle were an art form all their own.

Left
The Romans referred to the well-groomed appearance of the Celts, attested to by the neatly combed hair on the head depicted on the plaque. It dates from the 1st century AD.

Centre left
An enamelled bronze terret, or loop, for a horse's reins to pass through, found at Lesser Garth.

Below
The fragile remains of the Cerrigydrudion bronze bowl show the intricacy of early Celtic design and craftsmanship.

HILLFORTS AND WARRIORS

Right

An early Iron Age shield boss, part of the Llyn Cerrig Bach hoard of druidical votive offerings discovered when RAF Valley airfield on Anglesey was being laid in 1943. It is possible that the shield boss is one of the items left by Lindow Man.

Below

Pen-y-Gaer Iron Age hillfort, Llanbedr-y-Cennin, Conwy, has three ramparts and is noteworthy for having two areas of chevaux-de-frise, rows of sharp pointed stones, set in the ground facing the attacker – the Iron Age equivalent of barbed wire defences.

Nearly 600 Iron Age hillforts have been identified in Wales, evidence of the warlike nature of the ancient Celts. Some would have been refuges in times of trouble into which men and beasts could retreat when threatened, but many were the strongholds of chiefs who had the power to organize the immense labour forces needed to build them. Many thousands of tons of rock had to be broken down into large stones and manhandled into position to make walls hundreds of metres long. The bigger forts dominated large areas of the country, and within their walls accommodated town-size populations in as many as 150 stone huts. Some, dating from the Bronze Age, were rebuilt and extended with more elaborate defences several times over the centuries. Many were destroyed by enemy tribes, while others were used right through to the Roman occupation and beyond. They were massive structures with walls three metres thick and four or more metres high. The most elaborate part of the defensive system had to be the entrance, with in-turned or out-turned walls forming long narrow passages overlooked by a raised gate-house so that attackers would have to run the gauntlet of stones raining down upon them. A free-standing wall across the entrance to the passage prevented a concerted rush by the enemy. When roused, Celtic warriors assembled in their bands for battle quite openly and without forethought – 'they will face danger even if they have nothing but their own strength and courage'. So wrote the Greek geographer Strabo, and what he reported would apply to the Celts of Britain. Caesar was confronted by foot soldiers, cavalry and chariots. Foot soldiers were armed with long heavy slashing swords and small round shields. Some wore body armour and helmets, others only tunics and breeches. In the front row of battle the infantry were

often naked, their bodies covered with geometric patterns coloured with blue dye, and gold torques round their necks – rich booty for the Roman soldiers. The cavalry, which harried the enemy's flanks, were armed with spears and swords. The two-horse war chariot was used in Britain with great expertise; Caesar described them being driven about in all directions with warriors hurling javelins from on high, while the din of the wheels and the thunder of hooves spread disorder. In the midst of battle the warriors would jump down from the chariots and fight on foot, while the chariots were prudently withdrawn to positions that they could reach if hard pressed. They fought in random groupings, always with fresh reserves to change places. Horns and trumpets were sounded, more to put fear into the enemy than for signalling; there was little or no command structure but plenty of suicidal courage. The reputations of the chiefs and warriors were dependent on their successes in battle and tribal raids, and were confirmed in verse by the bards at the feasts which followed. At these the warriors were given the finest cuts of meat and vast quantities of wine and ale were drunk.

Below
Tre'r Ceiri on Yr Eifl, Lleyn Peninsula, is the most impressive of all British hillforts and also one of the highest. Within its walls, largely intact, are the remains of 150 stone huts.

Above
The 2½ mile wide Red Wharf Bay on Anglesey is overlooked by Bwrdd Arthur (Arthur's Seat), an early Iron Age hillfort with traces of the Romano-British occupation.

ulus Plautius invaded Britain in May 43 AD and in under three months had subdued the south east of the country. Within four years the northern frontier of the Roman empire was a line from Lincoln to Exeter, but it was a frontier under continuous attack by the tribes to the north and west. The most dangerous were the Silures of south-east Wales. Led by Caractacus (Caradog) who had fled to their territory after his defeat by Plautius, they fought two successful battles with the Romans in 47 and 48 AD, only to face defeat in 50 AD. Caractacus fled north where he was betrayed by the Queen of the Brigantes, ending up in chains in Rome. On the principle of divide and conquer, the Romans then drove a wedge between the tribes of the west country and those of south Wales, and another through the lowland gap of the Dee valley between the Brigantes and the Deceangli in what is now Denbighshire. The Celts of the Welsh peninsula were thus isolated from their cousins to the north and south, and were to remain so to the present day.

However, the unthinkable happened; the Silures revolted and defeated the 20th Legion, provoking Emperor Nero to order the complete subjugation of the British Isles. The first move in 60 AD was against the tribes of Wales – and Anglesey in particular, which was the granary of the highland Snowdonia – whom the Romans never could winkle out of their mountain stronghold. Anglesey was also

the power base of the Druids, implacable enemies of the Romans, who incited their warriors – men and women – to fight to the death. In 61 AD Suetonius Paulinus managed to get his army across the Menai Strait and massacred the Druids and burnt their sacred groves. The complete conquest of Wales was then postponed when he had to return east to subdue the bloody uprising of the Iceni led by Boudicca.

During the governorships of Julius Frontinus (74–78 AD) and Julius Agricola (78–84 AD) the conquest of Wales was given the highest priority. Three out of four legions in Britain were stationed on her borders at Caerleon in the south, at Wroxeter near Shrewsbury and at Chester. In all it took 13 campaigns to subdue the warlike Welsh tribes and impose a military occupation which lasted for 330 years. But it was never a total occupation; the Welsh conducted a continuous guerrilla warfare and many of the highland parts of the country remained no-go areas.

The fierce Silures were the first to come to terms with the Romans and moved out of their hillfort capital to found the civitas of Caerwent in Monmouthshire, a privilege granted by the Romans only to trusted tribes.

Few, apart from those in towns or settlements which grew up beside Roman forts, enjoyed any comforts of Roman culture. The Romans introduced other religions including Christianity, but by and large the tribes kept to the old gods. Celtic culture was diluted in Romanized England but remained largely intact in Wales. So too did the Celtic warrior spirit which was to serve them well in their long struggle against the Angles, Saxons, Vikings and, initially, the Norman kings, until the final conquest of the principality by Edward I and the death in 1283 of Llewelyn ap Gruffudd, Prince of Wales. This was the last of Celtic rule until Merlin's prophecy came true and the Welsh Tudors took the throne of England.

Above
One of the round huts in the fortified Celtic village of Din Lligwy on Anglesey which existed before, and survived, the Roman destruction of the Druids' island stronghold.

Many are the tales that are told of the days when Wales was ruled by kings whose knights were bold and chivalrous, slew dragons, rescued fair maidens, and defended their land against pagan invaders. Such tales passed into Welsh folklore, but they do have their historical connection with the Christian chieftains and military leaders who, in the dark years after the Romans left Britain, faced the onslaught of the pagan Jutes, Angles and Saxons. The greatest of them is said to have been King Arthur with his magician Merlin and the Knights of the Round Table. Whether he ever existed as one person or – more likely – is the personification of many leaders, we do not know, but his legend is a romanticized version of a period in history about which we have little other knowledge.

The first textual mention of Arthur is in *Historia Brittonum*, attributed to Nennius, a 9th-century Welsh monk. His name appears secondly in *Annales Cambriae* written in the 10th century and telling of his victory at Badon (variously dated between 490 and 518) and recording that he was killed at the Battle of Camlan(n) in either 515 or 539, depending on reference sources. The stories of the *Mabinogion*, written down in

Main picture
Craig-y-Ddinas in Vale of Neath where, according to one legend, King Arthur and his knights lie sleeping.

Right
Castell Dinas Bran in Denbighshire stands at a height of 308m above Llangollen. It was originally an Iron Age fort.

Far right
St Govan's Chapel in Pembrokeshire is a primitive stone hut thought to date from the 6th century. There are claims that St Govan was actually Sir Gawain, one of Arthur's knights.

the 14th and 15th centuries but told orally centuries before, have many references to Arthur and his Knights. Oral legend tells us that there was a great Celtic chief who led the 6th-century Britons against the Angles and Saxons and won many victories. Excavations of hillforts in north and south Wales have provided considerable, though not definite, proof that there was such a leader who came out of what is now Wales. Both Nennius and the *Mabinogion* talk of Caerleon 'City of the Legions' as being the site of King Arthur's Court and the Round Table, a romantic metamorphosis for the great Roman amphitheatre. It would certainly have made a good rallying place for a king and his warriors.

Whoever he was, Arthur is now an integral part of Welsh culture and the legends surrounding him have added drama and romance to the grandeur of the Welsh landscape.

Far left
The stone burial chamber at Reynoldston features in stories about King Arthur. A healing well springs up inside the chamber.

Left
Another view of Castell Dinas Bran where, legend says, the Holy Grail is buried. The castle has been a picturesque ruin since 1578.

As the Romans were leaving Britain, the west coast of Wales was subjected to attacks by the Goidel-speaking Celts from Ireland. The southern Irish tribes invaded and colonized the Pembrokeshire peninsula. Others, from the middle of Ireland, invaded the area now known as Gwynedd but were driven out by the Sons of Cunedda, a Celtic tribe from Northumberland who had settled in the north east of Wales at the invitation of the Romans, to act as a buffer between them and the unsubdued highland tribes of Snowdonia. They occupied the north of the country, and Cunedda's descendants became medieval princes of Wales with their court at Deganwy on the Conwy estuary. Meanwhile, in the south west, an Irish dynasty of princes was established which ruled until the 10th century.

At the same time another Irish invasion was taking place, that of the Irish missionaries who were to be the organizers of the early church in Wales. The roots of Christianity had been planted by the Romans but, apart from the south east, had hardly taken hold in the rest of the country and, as in England, faded out after the Romans left. The economy collapsed and there would be no place for a Roman church with worldly bishops and wealthy monasteries. The monks from Ireland, in tune with the times, retreated to remote places to live like hermits or congregated in monasteries under an abbot. The monks were few in number, and much of the proselytising was done by their lay disciples. The country had reverted to the old Celtic structure of innumerable tribal chiefs fighting among

themselves to increase their power bases and gain the most productive land. It was a dangerous time to be preaching Christian virtues, but those early missionaries gradually won over the chiefs by the example of their ascetic and disciplined lives. They were called 'sancti' by the monk historian Gildas in his monumental work *De Excidio Britanniae* ('The Destruction of

Britain'), written in 540. His 'sancti' came to be translated as 'saint', hence the Dark Ages in Wales became known as the Age of the Saints.

The Celtic saints, of whom there are substantial records, had a profound influence on early Welsh history. It was they who built monasteries, hospices and churches, became the councillors of princes, and were accredited with miraculous healing powers. Each became a cult in his own right with dedications over a wide area and the veneration of places connected with them and their relics. The cult of each saint related to the area of Wales in which he and his disciples had worked. Clynnog Fawr on the Lleyn Peninsula was the centre of St Beuno's cult which spread across the coastal areas of north Wales and Anglesey.

Above

The Houelt Cross stands in St Illtud's Church, Llantwit Major, Vale of Glamorgan, one of the oldest Christian sites in Britain.

Below

The 6th-century Bodvocus Stone in the Margam Stones Museum.

St Deiniol was venerated in the extreme east around Bangor-on-Dee, and St Tylio in the south in Powys centring on his church at Meifod. St Padarn's cult was in mid Wales, and in the south several cults overlapped with each other and that of St David. St Illtud, the father of the Welsh saints, founded his monastery and school c.500 AD at Llantwit Major in the Vale of Glamorgan, an area which had been well Romanized. His school, which has been called the first British university, was the seat of learning of the early Celtic church and numbered Samson, Gildas and David among its pupils. The school continued until the arrival of the Normans, and the monastery until the Dissolution. The church now standing on the site dates from around 1100 and contains an important collection of Celtic crosses.

The sites of early Celtic churches can often be identified by place names beginning with the prefix 'llan', meaning 'an enclosure'. It became the custom for chiefs and local nobles to donate a plot of land on which to have a sacred enclosure where the Christians could bury their dead. Often, later, a church was built on the site and St Bueno's church at Pistyll on the Lleyn Peninsula is a charming example, as is St Cynog's at Llangynog, Carmarthenshire, with its perfectly circular stone-walled churchyard. The traveller in Wales can find many such places by hunting out small churches in relatively isolated locations.

Another indication of an early church is the prefix 'Merthyr' to a place name, meaning 'relic'. These reliquaries, most often stones, crosses and holy wells, are to be found all over Wales and are part of the 'Cult of the Saints' which pervaded Welsh life between the 4th and 8th centuries. The cult is consistent with the folk memory of holy men who, being more learned than others, knew how to heal the sick, and when they succeeded, it might well have been a miracle. Holy wells

are to be found in churchyards and villages throughout Wales for the very good reason that no community, religious or secular, would build on a site that had no natural water supply. When a church was dedicated to a saint so was its well. An easy one to find, right beside the road opposite the church in Clynnog Fawr, was believed to have great healing powers up until quite recent times, but it was a kill or cure treatment. After bathing in the well, the patient had to lie all night on the cold slab of St Beuno's tomb.

Wales is well endowed with Christian monuments in the form of inscribed stones, gravestones and stone crosses dating from the 5th century. Most are inscribed in Latin, still the language of scholarship, others in Latin and Ogham or only Ogham. Later inscriptions were in Brythonic, and then in early Welsh which developed from it. The earliest example, inscribed in 650 AD, can be seen in St Cadfan's church in the seaside resort of Tywyn. St Cadfan arrived there from Brittany with his disciples in 516 and his holy well became famous for its healing powers.

Left
The 14th-century
church of St Tysilio on
Church Island, Menai
Bridge. It was founded
in the 7th century by
Tysilio, a son of the
royal house of Powys.

The Celtic church adhered to the rituals of the Western church as laid down in 314. After St Augustine was sent to England by Pope Gregory the Great in 597 to establish the see of Canterbury, he asked the Welsh church in 603 to join him in converting the pagan Anglo-Saxons. The Welsh declined, considering the church of Rome to be inferior to their own. Furthermore, they had no wish to come under the jurisdiction of Canterbury, which would be subject to the influence of their potential enemies, the Anglo-Saxons. So the church in Wales remained relatively isolated from the rest of Christianity for the next 165 years. During this time her Latin scholarship deteriorated, which was unfortunate but may have had the effect of forcing the development of the Welsh language. The church in Wales finally submitted to Rome in 768. It was to mark the beginning of the end of the Celtic church but not of Celtic religious art forms. These can be seen on many fine monuments of later dates, and the many forms of the Celtic cross are used even to this day, a legacy which can be found in churchyards throughout Britain.

Right
The late-9th or 10th-century Conbelin cross at the Margam Stones Museum.

Left
The holy well at Llangelynin Old Church above Conwy has been credited with miraculous healing powers from early Celtic times until recent years. Founded by St Celynin in the 7th century, the church is still used for worship.

LATE CELTIC ART

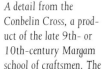

Right and below
A 6th–7th century
brooch from Anglesey
and an 8th-century
brooch found in north-
west Wales are both in
the Irish tradition of
Celtic art.

The threads of continuity of Celtic art running through the Dark Ages, the early Christian church and right through to the Norman conquest are found in the innumerable Christian monuments and memorials to rulers throughout Wales. At first between the 5th and 7th centuries they were crudely incised undressed stones covering graves or standing stones erected at holy sites and important trackways. Many carried abbreviated Latin inscriptions. Most interesting are those with incised figures, childlike in their execution but bearing a strong resemblance to the figures of gods and goddesses found on pre-Roman Celtic monuments.

The beautifully carved round-, disc- and wheel-headed crosses and pillar crosses did not appear in Wales until the 9th century, after the Welsh church had submitted to the church of Rome, but when they did the old style of Celtic graphics were often incorporated. Their surfaces, now worn almost smooth by centuries of weathering, were originally chisel sharp and highly coloured in reds, greens, blues and ochres. These monuments would have been carved by itinerant craftsmen, but there is evidence that from the 9th century Wales had a number of schools of sculpture or workshops under the patronage of wealthy churches and princely families. The Welsh royal courts were the social,

Right and below
A detail from the
Conbelin Cross, a prod-
uct of the late 9th- or
10th-century Margam
school of craftsmen. The
disc-headed cross-slab
from Llangan, West
Glamorgan is of the
same date.

political and cultural centres of the country. They were not in fixed locations, but each kingdom and principality – and there were many – had a number of centres around which the ruler and his retinue circulated.

Within a fort or stockade was a hall, the centre of public life, where the court would eat, drink and listen to poets and musicians. It was an heroic age of struggle against the Angles and Saxons and later the Vikings which stimulated verse, prose and music by the early medieval bards.

The harp and the Welsh crwth were the high art instruments of princely and aristocratic music. The latter was a development of the lyre with an added fingerboard and a bow, requiring a combination of plucking and bowing. One Iolo Gosh wrote a long poem on harps in the 14th century in which he saw the Welsh harp as being made of wood with black horse-hair strings. In those days harps were small, standing about a metre high when rested on the calves with ankles crossed. The tall harp resting on the floor did not reach Wales until the end of the 16th century. The wind instrument of the time was the pibgorn or Welsh hornpipe with bells of cow horn acting as amplifiers. With a range of only an octave, it suited the highly structured music of Wales. To play it required circular breathing – inflating the cheeks to supply pressure through the reed while continuing to breathe through the nose.

Being a poet or musician was a relatively easy life, lived in the comfort of patrons' houses, and in the early 15th century, at a meeting called an 'eisteddfod', an attempt was made to curb the growing number of second-rate travellers and minstrels who were bringing the bardic profession into disrepute. A further meeting in 1523 arranged for poets and musicians to be examined and graded by rank and status, but by then the days of princely patronage were ending and the bards were relegated to entertaining in inns and taverns.

Below
Dinas Emrys (the fort of Emrys) near Beddgelert, Gwynedd, dates from the 5th or 6th century. Its defences are a rare example of a totally post-Roman hillfort.

LITERATURE AND LANGUAGE

Main picture
*Legend has it that
Arthur assembled his
knights in the Brecon
Beacons, and the dip
between Pen-y-Fan and
Carn Du is known as
Arthur's Chair. Llan-
gorse Lake was known
for its prophetic powers
and was sacred to the
pagan Celts.*

With the collapse of the Roman empire and the demise of classical writers, Britain entered a dark age as far as recorded history is concerned. The Celts had no written language, and Brythonic was a long way from becoming the Welsh language as we know it. In the years between 400 and 600 AD the literature of Wales was a continuation of the oral tradition inherited from druidical days. It was an heroic era with princes vying with each other for land and power while at the same time embroiled in the struggle against the pagan Angles and Saxons. Early Welsh literature consisted of poems of praise and celebration of the warrior aristocracy and their victories, and lamentations over battles lost and leaders killed. They were committed to memory and recounted from one generation to another with varying degrees of accuracy and modification until they came to be written in manuscript form from the 9th century onwards, being copied many times and often edited in

...e process. It is therefore difficult to ...dge what was fact and what poetic ...cence, and how much pure myth was ...bsequently offered as historical fact by ...ter medieval writers.

The first written record of note was ...e *Excidio Britanniae* written in Latin by the ...rythonic monk and Latin author Gildas ...a c.547 AD. The Latin of the early Celtic ...hurch was in decline from the classical ...nguage and Gildas wrote in an eccentric ...orm mixed with Brythonic, Hebrew and ...reek called Hisperic, in which several ...exts were produced around the 7th ...entury. It was soon after Gildas completed his work that the Welsh language started to emerge from the Brythonic, although it was probably the 9th century before it came to be a written language.

At the end of the 8th century Welsh had ousted Latin as the language of the aristocracy. *Canu Heledd* ('The Song of Heledd'), a lament for the fall of the royal house of Powys in 855, was written in 'englyn', the oldest recorded Welsh metrical form. Welsh literature in its own language had arrived, and it has provided a strong sense of nationhood right through to the present day.

Below, inset
Left: *An early example of stone carving in Welsh, St Cadfan's Church, Tywyn.*
Centre: *A 6th-century memorial stone inscribed in Latin and Ogham at St Llawdog's Church, Cilgerran.*
Right: *The 5th–6th century Sagranus Stone in St Thomas's Church, St Dogmael's, near Cardigan, is inscribed in Latin and Ogham and provided the key for deciphering Ogham in 1848.*

Right

Bardsey Island, 2 miles off the tip of the Lleyn Peninsula, was an important place of pilgrimage from the 5th or 6th century onwards.

Below

Detail from the 11th-century Carew Cross, Pembrokeshire. A panel carries an inscription in round half-uncial, a new style of rounded letters established by the 7th century. The cross itself is of composite construction; its cross-head is attached to the shaft by a tenon joint.

◆ **Bardsey Island** off tip of Lleyn Peninsula, Gwynedd. A place of pilgrimage during the early years of the Celtic church and later. Tradition says it was the burial place of saints. It can be reached by tripper boat from Aberdaron in good weather. There are few visible remains.

◆ **Briamail's Cross,** Llanefaelog Fach, Powys. A 10th-century 2.5m long cross-slab depicting a figure holding a club and dagger.

◆ **Bryn Myrddin** (Merlin's Hill) near Abergwili, Carmarthenshire. One of many places that claim to be where Merlin sleeps.

◆ **Caerau** near Cardiff. A hillfort with three ramparts around a plateau, one of the strongest forts in south Wales.

◆ **Caer Gybi,** Anglesey. A Roman fort where St Cybi founded a church in the 6th century.

◆ **Caer Leb** near Llanidan, Anglesey. Slight remains of small 3rd-century settlement defended by a ditch.

◆ **Caerleon** near Newport. Best known for its Roman fort, town walls, baths and the best-preserved Roman amphitheatre in the country. It has a strong connection with early Celtic Christianity and the Arthurian legend. A bishop of Caerleon attended the Synod of Arles in France in 314 AD which was the first council of western Christianity. Geoffrey of Monmouth in his *History of the Kings of Britain* in 1136 wrote that King Arthur lived and was crowned in Caerleon, and that the amphitheatre was the Round Table at which his knights assembled, and so started one of the long-lasting legends about King Arthur. The small town has a Legionary Museum with artefacts and information on the Romano-Celts of the area.

◆ **Caerwent** east of Newport. Substantial remains including impressive walls of the original town, Venta Silurum, built by the Romans as a capital for the Celtic Silures tribe in 76 AD when they were moved from their hillfort Llanmelin a mile to the north. It became a prosperous civilian town of Romanized Celts. The forum is currently being excavated.

◆ **Caer y Twr,** Anglesey. An Iron Age fort on summit of Holyhead Mountain partially destroyed by Romans. Some stone ramparts still stand 3m high.

◆ **Caldey Island,** Pembrokeshire. Reached by boat from Tenby, it is owned by the Cistercians. The island's Welsh name is Ynys Pyr after the first Celtic abbot of a monastery founded in the 5th century. St David's church nearby dates from the 8th century. The church of St Illtyd houses a pillar stone inscribed in 5th-century Ogham and 9th-century Latin asking people to pray for the soul of Cadogan.

◆ **Carew Cross,** west of Tenby, Pembrokeshire. Magnificent 4m high Celtic cross erected in memory of Maredudd ap Edwin, a Welsh prince killed in 1035. Its interwoven patterns show Celtic and Viking influences.

◆ **Carmarthen.** Its Welsh name is Caerfyrddin, and legend has it that

Merlin (Fryddin) was born in the town, the grandson of a king. A priory once stood on the site of St Peter's church and it was there that the *Black Book of Carmarthen*, the oldest existing manuscript in Welsh, was written in the 12th century. It is now in the National Library, Aberystwyth.

◆ **Castell Henllys** near Nevern, Pembrokeshire. An Iron Age-cum-Romano British hillfort, being excavated. There are reconstruction round huts, granaries and implements.

◆ **Castell Odo,** Lleyn Peninsula, Gwynedd. Site of 3rd-century BC Iron Age settlement with double bank defences and signs of round huts.

◆ **Catamanus Stone,** Llangadwaladr Church, Anglesey. Post-Roman memorial with Latin inscription to Cadfan, d.625.

◆ **Clwydian Hills.** A line of rounded summits running parallel with the Ruthin–Denbigh road topped by four Iron Age hillforts. The highest of them is on Moel Fenlli (511m) which can be reached from Llanbedr on the Ruthin–Mold road. The others are all within walking distance of lanes leading off the B5429 starting at Llanbedr and running north. None has substantial remains.

◆ **Clynnog Fawr,** Gwynedd. St Beuno founded a church here c.616, but the present church is early16th-century. Adjoining it is St Beuno's Chapel which houses his tomb where miracles were claimed.

◆ **Conwy Mountain,** Conwy. An Iron Age fort with about 60 round hut foundations surrounded by a rampart.

◆ **Craig Gwrtheyrn.** Hillfort with contour stone defences above the river Teifi outside Llanysul, Carmarthenshire. Interesting for *chevaux-de-frise.*

◆ **Craig Rhiwarth** near Llangynog, Powys. An Iron Age hillfort site with the remains of 150 stone huts.

◆ **Din Lligwy** near Moelfre, Anglesey. An excellent site of a small Romano-British Celtic settlement with round and square stone huts and workshops. It is surrounded by defensive stone walling.

◆ **Dinas Emrys,** Gwynedd. A fort site on the south side of Snowdon above the Beddgelert–Llyn Dinas road. Insubstantial remains, but excavations around a manmade pool, dating from

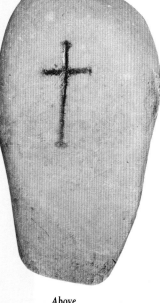

Above
A stone incised with a cross, said to have been made by St Beuno when he was given a grant of land on which to build his church at Clynnog Fawr on the Lleyn Peninsula in 630 AD. After bathing in his nearby holy well, the sick had to spend a night lying on his tombstone. The cult to the saint was centred on this site, from where it spread across north Wales and Anglesey.

the 1st or 2nd century AD, revealed a connection with Vortigern in the 5th century when he was campaigning against Ambrosius Aurelianus (Emrys).

◆ **Dyserth** near Llandrindod Wells, Powys. There is an interesting church where St Cewydd built his dwelling on a site used for Celtic worship. Its Celtic connection is manifested by its circular churchyard which would have been a typical Celtic burial ground.

◆ **Eliseg's Pillar and Cairn,** Denbighshire. A 2.5m high pillar close by the ruined abbey of Valle Crucis near Llangollen is of great historical importance to the Welsh. It was erected in the 9th century by Cyngan in memory of his great grandfather Eliseg, a king, who annexed Powys from the English. Civil War vandalism and centuries of weathering have destroyed the lettering and the crosshead is missing, but the cairn on which it stands was found to contain remains thought to be those of a chief; his skull was gilded before reburial as a sign of respect to an ancestor of the Powys line.

◆ **Fynnon Gybi,** Llangybi, Gwynedd. A healing well 5 miles from Pwllheli with a pool dating back to the 6th century.

◆ **Garn Boduan,** Gwynedd. A large hillfort beside the Nefyn–Pwllheli road on the Lleyn Peninsula. Fortifications span two periods, the latter lasting to the 12th century. There are remains of 170 round huts within the 14 hectare site.

◆ **Garn Fadron** in the centre of the Lleyn Peninsula, Gwynedd, is a 5 hectare Iron Age hillfort reached from Garn village. The main ramparts

enclose some 10 hectares of the hilltop, and an inner defence encloses foundations of round huts.

◆ **Gower Peninsula,** near Swansea. Designated an Area of Outstanding Natural Beauty. There are five Iron Age hillforts – most on promontories, so naturally defended on three sides – and Minchin Hole, a coastal cave occupied from the pre-Roman Iron Age through to the 7th century.

◆ **Holywell,** Flintshire. St Beuno built a chapel here in the 7th century. Soon afterwards his sister or niece, Winefride, was threatened by Caradoc, a local priest. When she resisted him he decapitated her; where her head fell a spring bubbled up and the site became a place of pilgrimage.

◆ **Llanmelin Wood,** Newport. 150 BC hillfort which was strengthened in 50 BC and may have been the tribal capital of the Silures before they occupied the civitas of Caerwent.

Above

St Winefride's Well, Holywell, Flintshire, is the most important holy well in Britain, and has been a place of pilgrimage since the 7th century.

Right

The Gower Peninsula stretches for 14 miles from Mumbles Head on Swansea Bay to its tip at Worms Head. It is an area of outstanding natural beauty and rich in sites of historical interest, including churches and Iron Age hillforts.

◆ **Llantwit Major** in the Vale of Glamorgan. One of the oldest Christian sites in Britain. St Illtud founded a monastery and school here around 500 AD. The west church was built on the site of the original in about 1100 and extended by the east church in the 14th century. Several Celtic stones in the west church suggest there was a school of sculpture there in the pre-Norman era.

◆ **Llanwrthwl Church,** Powys. The 11th-century font in St Gwrthwl's church is carved with four heads projecting from its round bowl, and is considered to be an echo of the Celtic cult of the head.

◆ **Llyn y Fan Fach,** Powys. A beautiful little lake in the Black Mountains connected with the legend of the Lady of the Lake who brought magic and white cows as her dowry but returned to her lake world after being struck with iron three times by her husband.

The legend illustrates the fear the old order had of the skilled ironworkers.

◆ **Machynlleth,** Powys. **Celtica**, a recently opened interpretive centre provides an audio-visual journey back in time to the ancient Celts. Also, at the Corris Craft Centre, **King Arthur's Labyrinth**, an exhibition in old mining caverns, displaying the legends of Arthur.

◆ **Maen Achwyfan,** Flintshire. A 10th-century Northumbrian-style cross with Viking and Celtic influence in the designs on the shaft. It stands in a field a mile from Whitford.

◆ **Manorbier,** Pembrokeshire. Best known as the birthplace of Giraldus (1146–1223) who travelled through Wales with Archbishop Baldwin and wrote *Itinerarium Cambriae* from which comes much of our knowledge of life in Wales in his period. Manorbier Castle is open to the public.

◆ **Nash Point Fort,** near Llantwit Major, Vale of Glamorgan. Four ramparts and ditches are visible, but nothing remains within them.

◆ **Nevern,** Pembrokeshire. The Great Cross of St Brynach stands in the churchyard. Dating from the 10th century and elaborately patterned, it is 4m high and one of the most perfect Celtic crosses in Wales. Near the porch is the Vitalianus Stone, bearing both Latin and Ogham inscriptions. Two more, the Magloconus Stone and the Cross Stone, now form window-sills in the church, the latter bearing a Viking pattern.

◆ **Old Oswestry** near Oswestry, Shropshire. The most impressive of the Iron Age hillforts in the Marches, but this is only apparent from the air.

◆ **Pen Dinas,** Ceredigion. An Iron Age hillfort south of Aberystwyth has twin summits which were individually fortified and then further protected by

Above
The Maen Achwyfan Cross (Stone of Lamentations) was erected c.1000 on the roadside near Whitford, Flintshire, and is particularly well preserved. It is a disc-headed cross-slab, and the style of its decoration is related to that on Northumbrian crosses.

Above
A cross of c.1000 at Penmon Priory.

Below
A burial stone at Penmachno with a Latin inscription meaning 'Oria Lies Here'. Inscribed stones such as this are the earliest archaeological evidence of Christianity in north Wales.

a single defensive wall. It is believed to have been occupied for some 300 years up to and including the 1st century BC.

◆ **Penmachno,** near Betws-y-Coed, Conwy. There is a small church which houses one of the best collections of early Celtic Christian stones in Wales. One is inscribed with the Chi-Rho monogram for Christ; others inscribed in Latin and dating from the 5th and 6th centuries indicated a continuing Roman influence after the departure of the Legions.

◆ **Penmon**, Anglesey. The Priory was founded by St Seiriol in the 6th century. Parts of the ruins, his holy well, cell and the monks' fishpond can still be seen. He also founded a church on Puffin Island just off shore: there are scant remains.

◆ **Pen-y-Corddin,** Conwy. One of the biggest Iron Age hillforts in north Wales is a rock mass standing on the coastal plain south west of Abergele which needed little in the way of artificial defences, its main defence being the precipitous escarpment on all but the north approach. Traces of huts can be seen aerially, but are not readily discernible on the ground.

◆ **Pen-y-Gaer,** Powys. A small hillfort by Llyn Clywedog reservoir north west of Llanidloes. The remains of the outer stone wall and an overlapping entrance can be discerned.

◆ **Pen-y-Gaer,** Conwy. A hillfort south of Conwy, it is a particularly interesting site with the ruins of two stone ramparts and *chevaux-de-frise*, but scant signs of huts and iron workshops. It is a natural defensive site with magnificent views.

◆ **St David's,** Pembrokeshire. A small cathedral city with the finest church in Wales. Tradition says a cell was founded there by St David in 550 AD: the present building dates from only 1180. There are several inscribed

Celtic stones and wheel-crosses from the 9th and 10th centuries.

◆ **St David's Peninsula** from St David's Head to Solva is an area rich in prehistoric remains, the two most identifiable being Clawdd y Milwyr, an Iron Age promontory fort, and Clegyr Boia, with the remains of an Iron Age dwelling and traces of a neolithic farm, possibly of Irish origin.

◆ **St Non's Chapel**, Pembrokeshire. A ruin on the clifftop above St Non's Bay. It is c.7th century and is an example of the earliest church building in Wales. Legend says St David, son of St Non, was born here.

◆ **Skomer Island,** off Pembrokeshire coast. Covered with the remains of Iron Age huts and walled cultivation sites. The huts are both round and rectangular and dated around the 1st century BC. The island is under the management of the Dyfed Wildlife Trust and can be visited by boat.

◆ **Strata Florida Abbey**, north east of Lampeter, Carmarthenshire. Founded by the Cistercians in 1164, but the ruins are of the 12th-century church which for 200 years was the religious, political and academic centre of Wales. It was here that Llewelyn the Great called an assembly of Welsh princes in 1238 to swear allegiance to his son Dafydd.

◆ **Tredegar Camp**, Newport. The ramparts of an Iron Age hillfort surround a medieval motte and bailey.

◆ **Tre'r Ceiri**, Gwynedd. The most impressive hillfort site in Wales, on the Lleyn Peninsula. The remains of some 50 huts can still be seen. The site is topped by a Bronze Age cairn.

◆ **Ty Mawr**, Anglesey. Iron Age settlement at the foot of Holyhead Mountain near South Stack. Substantial remains can be seen of 20 out of 50 original circular huts. Excavations have shown that it was inhabited during the Roman occupation of Britain.